The Ultimate Guide to Pricing

For Accountants & Bookkeepers

by

Johann Goree

Legal Disclaimer

This book is provided solely for informational and educational purposes to help accounting and bookkeeping firms establish their own pricing strategies. It is not intended to set or dictate pricing standards for any business or service. The suggestions and formulas included herein are based on general industry research, personal experience, and survey data but should be used as a framework, not as mandatory or prescriptive pricing guidelines.

The author and Engager.app strictly comply with UK anti-competition laws and regulations. As such, no specific prices, fixed fees, or pricing structures are mandated or endorsed within this book. Readers are encouraged to develop independent pricing methods based on their unique business requirements, client bases, and service offerings. Any resemblance between suggested ranges and individual firm rates is coincidental and intended only to illustrate industry trends.

The content of this book should not be construed as financial, legal, or professional advice, and it may not be suitable for every firm's unique circumstances. We recommend consulting a qualified legal professional or business advisor before implementing any pricing strategies to ensure compliance with all applicable laws and regulations.

Dedication

To my wife,

Thank you for your endless patience, understanding, and for tolerating the countless weekends and evenings I spend buried in my work, including this book, instead of being fully present with you. Your support and love have been my anchor, and this book wouldn't exist without your ability to forgive the late-night typing sessions and distractions of my work.

To my Dad and late Mum,

Your belief and support has always been unwavering. Thank you for teaching me that I can achieve anything I set my mind to and for cheering me on at every step of the journey. Your morals, advice and encouragement have been the foundation for everything I do.

Table of Contents

"Using this guide alongside Engager will transform your practice to make sure you're maximising your prices."

- Alan Meikle, Balance Master Account Services

"Excellent clear and concise guide for anyone starting out on their pricing journey. Thank you, Johann"

- Matthew Portess, Appleleaf Accountancy

About the Author

With over seven years of hands-on experience running a group of accounting and bookkeeping firms and two years in Engager.app, Johann Goree, Co-Founder, Head of Growth & Community at Engager.app, brings a wealth of practical knowledge and experience to this guide.

Johann is a committed advocate for the UK Accounting and Bookkeeping profession having spent years working, reading, researching, and experimenting with pricing strategies that work in his own firm and the real world.

He has become a well-known figure within the UK Accounting and Bookkeeping community speaking at events and on webinars about many different topics, but the underlaying theme to them all is his openness and honesty about what has and hasn't worked.

Johann's journey through the complexities of both practice management and pricing, along with the insights gathered from conversations with Engager's community of accounting and bookkeeping professionals, has driven him to create practical solutions for today's practice management and pricing challenges.

Now, through Engager.app, Johann aims to share those insights, helping firms develop pricing models that are reflective of the unique value they bring to clients.

- Ash Hall, Head of Product, Engager.app

Introduction

Before diving into this book, I want to set the scene with some context and advice.

First and foremost, this is just a book designed to help accountants and bookkeepers to create and logic-test their own pricing. It is **not** a "do it this way or you're wrong" type of book, nor does it mean you will fail if you do not follow it exactly. We all price and run our businesses differently based on the clients we serve, and that is completely okay—in fact, in my humble opinion, it's exactly what the Accounting and Bookkeeping industry needs!

This book has been structured with your priorities in mind. The practical answers to "how to price"—the reason you picked up this book—are right at the beginning, so you can dive straight into the actionable content. Following that, you'll find the theories, insights, and strategies that underpin those pricing methods and approaches. While I hope you'll read beyond the "how to" section to fully benefit from the broader context, I understand that many of you are here for the immediate answers. I've intentionally avoided burying the key information amidst layers of theory because, like you, I find it frustrating when authors or business coaches hide the solutions they promise on the cover deep within the content. This book was created to be as straightforward and practical as possible, right from the start

This book is built on experience and knowledge from seven years of running my own Accounting & Bookkeeping firms, countless hours of reading books and articles, attending webinars, and participating in in-person sessions focused on pricing strategies. I have also spoken about pricing at events and on webinars over the years.

To complete this book I have combined those insights gained along with recent research I have carried out within the Engager.app Community.

Engager's goal is to ensure that by using our pricing calculator, combined with Letters of Engagement designed by you using the Document Designer, you will gain the confidence to charge fees that reflect your value—allowing your clients to clearly see the benefit of working with you.

While this book is tailored with Engager.app's Practice Management software in mind, the methods and theories discussed can be applied to any pricing platform—even something as simple as spreadsheets—if that's what works for you.

At the time of this book's publication, Engager.app is the fastest growing and award-winning practice management tool in the UK, with over 1,000 firms using it to price clients and run their practices efficiently. To learn more, visit www.Engager.app or join our Facebook community, *Practice Management Excellence by Engager.app*, where we have over 1,900 active users and followers.

The services outlined in this book are not exhaustive, and your firm might offer services beyond those discussed here. However, the principles shared should be adaptable enough to be applied across your offerings.

In the UK, giving exact prices or setting industry-standard rates would be in direct conflict with anti-competition laws, which are designed to keep the market fair and open. Compliance with these laws ensures that firms operate independently, allowing each to price their services based on their unique value, expertise, and costs. This book, therefore, doesn't provide fixed prices but rather a framework to help you establish your own tailored fees. The aim is to empower you to set prices that reflect the work and value you deliver to clients, without constraining your firm or infringing on these essential regulations. The flexibility of our examples and formulas is here to support you—not to dictate your rates.

The book is structured around Engager.app's capabilities, covering service types, price ranges, and Key Pricing Indicators (KPIs) to consider as you build and refine your pricing but can be applied in other pricing tools and practice management tools as well.

Register for a free trial of Engager

Key Terminology

While there's a detailed glossary at the back of this book, I wanted to define a few key terms before we delve into the detail of pricing:

Key Pricing Indicators (KPIs)

A Key Pricing Indicator (KPI) is a piece of information that influences the price of a service—such as the number of bank transactions, invoices, employees, annual turnover, or frequency of service.

Before you get excited and start planning an extravagant pricing model please remember, some Pricing software's limit you to the number of KPI's you can use per service, Engager.app allows unlimited KPI's so you can price your clients in any way you would like considering as many KPI's as you deem appropriate.

In my firm, we use *Xenon* to pull the numbers needed for pricing a client. Xenon provides quick, easy access to data like turnover, purchase invoices, sales invoices, and more, making fee reviews straightforward. There are other tools for this, like QuickBooks' built-in insights, Syft Analytics, Dext, and Xero's reporting features.

Other KPIs might include client ranking, AML risk levels, source of clients, software used, and quality of records. For instance, when assessing record quality, you might assign a multiplier of 1 for good records, 2 for poor, and 0.8 for excellent. This means good records are charged at your base rate, poor-quality records are priced higher, and excellent records receive a slight discount. These KPIs then adjust the **Base Rate** you've set for each service.

Base Rate (BR)

The Base Rate (BR) is your starting point—it's the amount you charge per document, month, or year for a given service. Think of it as the amount charged per payslip, tax return, or purchase invoice. Throughout this book, I'll share typical base rate ranges that firms are using, as well as the average rates.

Hourly and Daily Charge-Out Rates

In this book, I'll be focusing primarily on fixed-fee pricing and what firms are charging under this model. While hourly and daily rates aren't "wrong" by any means, they can limit earning potential because there are only so many hours you can work in a week. Fixed fees, on the other hand, allow for better scalability and incentivise implementing automations and tools to work more efficiently.

Some clients, some services, and some firms can only work on hourly or daily rates, and that's fine—Engager.app is designed to support this approach within its Letters of Engagement.

Pricing Equations

The pricing equations shared in this book are just examples. They're meant to be starting points, not rules. It's your business, so feel free to use parts of them, tweak them, or add your own variables on top.

Within Engager.app, you have two methods of pricing:

1. **Wizard Mode** for simpler pricing using linear calculations.
2. **Advanced Mode** that supports BODMAS (Brackets, Orders, Division and Multiplication, Addition, and Subtraction) calculations, like how spreadsheets work.

You can decide which method works best for your firm—service by service. If for any reason you aren't using Engager.app for pricing, you will need to check which calculation methods your tool supports before diving to deeply into this book.

Bookkeeping Services

Bookkeeping is often hard to define because its scope varies greatly depending on both the firms and the business owner's perspective. Some see it as including credit control, while others believe it starts after receipts are scanned into a processing software like AutoEntry, Apron, or Dext and stops once the data is entered into the bookkeeping software.

My advice is to break down the term "bookkeeping" into distinct service areas. This approach allows you to price accurately for each aspect of the service and ensures your client knows exactly what they're paying for in your Proposal or Letter of Engagement.

Breaking Down Bookkeeping Services

So, what do I mean by breaking down the Bookkeeping service? Think about the various tasks you perform for different clients and use those as a starting point. In my firm, to make it clear that each service is part of the broader bookkeeping function, we name them "Bookkeeping – [Service Area]." Below are some examples of how we've structured these services. Use these as a template to build on, adjust, or completely reinvent based on your own needs.

Bookkeeping - Processing Bank Transactions

This service involves processing each transaction on the bank feed. The goal is to automate as much as possible using rules or AI tools. Automation can reduce the amount you charge (due to time savings) or increase profitability by maintaining your fees while reducing manual input.

Typical Rates:

- Base rate: £0.15 to £1.50 per transaction (average: £1.00)

Pricing Factors:

- Average number of transactions
- Frequency of service (daily services are priced higher than weekly or monthly)
- Quality of records (poor-quality records incur higher fees)

Example Formula:

Base Rate x Average Number of Transactions x Frequency x Quality of Records = Monthly Fee

A table showing how these Key pricing Indicators impact the fees you charge is on the next page.

Example table:

Base Rate (£)	Avg. Transactions	Frequency Of Work	Quality of Records Multiplier	Monthly Fee (£)
0.15	100	1.0 (Monthly)	1.0 (Good)	15.00
1.00	250	1.2 (Fortnightly)	1.5 (Average)	450.00
1.50	500	1.5 (Weekly)	2.0 (Poor)	1500.00

Example Formula:

Base Rate x Average Number of Transactions x Frequency x Quality of Records = Monthly Fee

This table demonstrates how the monthly fee varies based on different base rates, average transaction counts, frequency multipliers, and quality of records multipliers.

Bookkeeping - Bank Reconciliation

This service involves reconciling bank accounts within bookkeeping software against bank statements. There are two common methods for pricing this: charging per transaction (as above) or charging a flat rate per bank account.

Typical Rates:

- Base rate: £7.50 to £20.00 per bank account/credit card (average: £15.00)

Pricing Factors:

- Number of accounts requiring reconciliation
- Frequency of service (monthly, quarterly, or annually)

Example Formula:

Base Rate x Number of Accounts x Frequency = Monthly Fee

A table showing how these Key pricing Indicators impact the fees you charge is on the next page.

Example table:

Base rate (£)	Number of Accounts	Frequency Of Work	Monthly Fee (£)
7.50	1	1.0 (Monthly)	7.50
15.00	3	1.0 (Monthly)	45.00
20.00	2	0.25 (Quarterly)	10.00
15.00	5	0.083 (Annually)	6.25

Example Formula:

Base Rate x Number of Accounts x Frequency = Monthly Fee

In this table:

- The "Frequency Multiplier" reflects the service interval: 1.0 for monthly, 0.25 for quarterly, and 0.083 for annually.
- The "Monthly Fee" is calculated by multiplying the base rate, the number of accounts, and the frequency multiplier, giving a straightforward view of potential charges based on varying service levels.

Bookkeeping - Processing Purchase Invoices

This service covers processing each receipt or purchase invoice. Ideally, you should use document processing software with Optical Character Recognition (OCR) technology to extract amounts, dates, suppliers, and other details. Automation can help increase profitability by reducing manual work.

Typical Rates:

- Base rate: £0.35 to £1.00 per transaction (average: £0.75)

Pricing Factors:

- Average number of purchase invoices/receipts
- Frequency of service (daily services are priced higher than weekly or monthly)
- Quality of records (poor-quality records incur higher fees)

Example Formula:

Base Rate x Average Number of Purchase Invoices/Receipts x Frequency x Quality of Records = Monthly Fee

A table showing how these Key pricing Indicators impact the fees you charge is on the next page.

Example table:

Base Rate (£)	Avg. Number of Inv/Rec	Frequency Of Work	Quality of Records Multiplier	Monthly Fee (£)
0.35	100	1.0 (Daily)	1.5 (Poor)	52.50
0.75	200	0.5 (Weekly)	1.0 (Average)	75.00
1.00	150	0.25 (Monthly)	0.8 (Excellent)	30.00
0.75	300	1.0 (Daily)	1.2 (Below Average)	270.00

Example Formula:

Base Rate x Average Number of Purchase Invoices/Receipts x Frequency x Quality of Records = Monthly Fee

In this table:

- Frequency Multiplier reflects the service interval: 1.0 for daily, 0.5 for weekly, and 0.25 for monthly.
- Quality of Records Multiplier adjusts for record quality: 1.5 for poor, 1.2 for below average, 1.0 for average, and 0.8 for excellent.

- Monthly Fee is calculated by multiplying the base rate, the average number of invoices/receipts, the frequency multiplier, and the quality of records multiplier.

Bookkeeping - Processing Sales Invoices

This service is like processing purchase invoices but involves sales invoices. Sales invoices typically require more time, and there's often less automation available, which is why higher rates are usually charged.

Typical Rates:

- Base rate: £2.50 to £7.50 per transaction (average: £5.00)

Pricing Factors:

- Average number of sales invoices
- Frequency of service (daily services are priced higher than weekly or monthly)
- Quality of records (poor-quality records incur higher fees)

Example Formula:

Base Rate x Average Number of Sales Invoices x Frequency x Quality of Records = Monthly Fee

A table showing how these Key pricing Indicators impact the fees you charge is on the next page.

Example table:

Base Rate (£)	Avg. Number of Sales Invoices	Frequency Of Work	Quality of Records Multiplier	Monthly Fee (£)
2.50	50	1.0 (Daily)	1.5 (Poor)	187.50
5.00	100	0.5 (Weekly)	1.0 (Average)	250.00
7.50	75.00	0.25 (Monthly)	0.8 (Excellent)	112.50
5.00	150	1.0 (Daily)	1.2 (Below Average)	900.00

Example Formula:

Base Rate x Average Number of Sales Invoices x Frequency x Quality of Records = Monthly Fee

In this table:

- Frequency Multiplier adjusts for service frequency: 1.0 for daily, 0.5 for weekly, and 0.25 for monthly.
- Quality of Records Multiplier reflects record quality: 1.5 for poor, 1.2 for below average, 1.0 for average, and 0.8 for excellent.

- Monthly Fee is calculated by multiplying the base rate, average number of sales invoices, frequency multiplier, and quality of records multiplier.

Bookkeeping - Credit Control

This service helps clients get paid faster by chasing overdue invoices. Various tools, like Adfin, Chaser, and Know-It, offer automated processes to help manage this.

Typical Rates:

- Base rate: £5.00 to £7.50 per invoice or customer chased (average: £5.00)

Pricing Factors:

- Average number of customers or invoices chased
- Frequency of service (daily services are priced higher than weekly or monthly)

Example Formula:

Base Rate x Average Number of Customers/Invoices Chased x Frequency = Monthly Fee

A table showing how these Key pricing Indicators impact the fees you charge is on the next page.

Example table:

Base Rate (£)	Avg. Number of Customers/Invoices Chased	Frequency Of Work	Monthly Fee (£)
5.00	20	1.0 (Daily)	100.00
7.50	15	0.5 (Weekly)	56.25
5.00	30	0.25 (Monthly)	37.50
6.00	50	1.0 (Daily)	300.00

Example Formula:

Base Rate x Average Number of Customers/Invoices Chased x Frequency = Monthly Fee

In this table:

- Frequency Multiplier reflects the service frequency: 1.0 for daily, 0.5 for weekly, and 0.25 for monthly.
- Monthly Fee is calculated by multiplying the base rate, average number of customers/invoices chased, and frequency multiplier.

VAT Service

VAT services are usually charged monthly, but some firms prefer to charge quarterly. One key KPI we see in VAT service pricing is **industry type**, where fees may fluctuate depending on the client's industry due to complexity or preference.

A second key pricing indicator used in this service pricing model which we haven't looked at yet is annual turnover, this is where firms charge fees based on the amount their client turns over in a given period, some look at monthly averages, quarterly or annually so the smaller clients pay less than the bigger clients normally because the volume of work increases with increased turnover.

Typical Rates:

- Base rate: £25.00 to £45.00 per month (average: £35.00)

Pricing Factors:

- Annual Turnover
- Frequency of service (Monthly, Quarterly, Annually)
- Industry Type

Example Formula:

Base Rate x Annual Revenue x Frequency x Industry Type = Monthly Fee

A table showing how these Key pricing Indicators impact the fees you charge is below.

Example table:

Base Rate (£)	Annual Turnover (Multiplier)	Frequency Of Work	Industry Type Multiplier	Monthly Fee (£)
35.00	1.2 (Mid-range)	1.0 (Quarterly)	1.1 (Complex Industry)	46.20
25.00	1.5 (High)	1.0 (Quarterly)	1.0 (Standard Industry)	9.38
45.00	1.0 (Low)	2.5 (Monthly)	1.3 (High Complexity)	146.25
30.00	1.4 (Mid-High)	0.083 (Annually)	1.0 (Standard Industry)	3.50

In this table:

- Annual Turnover Multiplier varies based on the client's revenue level.
- Frequency Multiplier reflects the billing frequency: 2.5 for monthly because we assume quarterly is the norm, 1 for quarterly, and 0.083 for annually.
- Industry Type Multiplier adjusts for industry complexity, with higher multipliers for more complex industries.

Payroll Services

Payroll is another service that can cover a broad spectrum of offerings. Breaking it down into smaller service components allows for more accurate pricing. I'll break them down as we did above for bookkeeping.

Payroll - Directors Only

This service is for companies where the Accountant or Bookkeeper only provides payroll for Directors. It's usually just a monthly payslip covering the Annual Tax-Free Allowance divided by twelve.

Typical Rates:

- Base rate: £5.00 to £25.00 per director (average: £17.00)

Pricing Factors:

- Number of directors

Example Formula:

Base Rate x Number of Directors = Monthly Fee

Payroll - Employee Payroll

This service covers the payroll for a business's employees, whether run weekly, fortnightly, or monthly. We typically see two methods used for pricing:

- A fixed amount per payslip, which often reduces as volume increases due to efficiency gains.
- A minimum fee per pay run, regardless of the number of payslips, plus a smaller amount per payslip.

Typical Rates:

- Base rate: £3.00 to £5.00 per payslip (average varies depending on volume and frequency)

Pricing Factors:

- Number of employees
- Frequency of payroll
- Pay type (hourly, salaried, etc.)

Example Formula:

Base Rate x Number of Employees x Pay Type = Monthly Fee

A table showing how these Key pricing Indicators impact the fees you charge is on the next page.

Example table:

Base Rate (£)	Number of Employees	Frequency Of Work	Pay Type	Monthly Fee (£)
4.00	10	1.0 (Monthly)	1.0 (Salaried)	40.00
5.00	25	Fortnightly (1.5)	1.5 (Hourly)	281.25
3.50	15	2.0 (Weekly)	1.0 (Salaried)	105.00
4.50	20	1.0 (Monthly)	1.5 (Hourly)	135.00
3.00	30	1.0 (Monthly)	1.0 (Salaried)	90.00

Example Formula:

Base Rate x Number of Employees x Pay Type = Monthly Fee

In this table:

- Base Rate varies depending on volume efficiency and chosen pricing method.
- Number of Employees affects the calculation based on workforce size.

- Frequency (weekly, fortnightly, monthly) influences the total payroll workload.
- Pay Type (hourly, salaried) can add complexity, influencing rates.

Pension Submissions

While many firms include this in their payroll fee, more firms are starting to charge separately, making their payroll offering more affordable for businesses that don't have employees on a pension scheme.

Typical Rates:

- Base rate: £2.50 to £5.00 per employee on a pension (average: £5.00)

Pricing Factors:

- Number of employees enrolled in the pension
- Frequency of pension submissions
- Pension provider (some are easier to work with than others)

Example Formula:

Base Rate x Number of Employees on Pension x Pension Provider = Monthly Fee

A table showing how these Key pricing Indicators impact the fees you charge is on the next page.

Example table:

Base Rate (£)	Number of Employees on Pension	Frequency Of Work	Pension Provider	Monthly Fee (£)
3.00	5	1.0 (Monthly)	1.0 (Provider A)	15.00
4.50	10	2.0 (Weekly)	1.5 (Provider B)	135.00
5.00	8	1.5 (Fortnightly)	1.0 (Provider A)	60.00
2.50	12	1.0 (Monthly)	2.0 (Provider C)	60.00
4.00	15	2.0 (Weekly)	1.5 (Provider B)	180.00

Example Formula:

Base Rate x Number of Employees on Pension x Pension Provider = Monthly Fee

In this table:

- Frequency (weekly, fortnightly, monthly) affects how often submissions are made, impacting the fee.
- Pension Provider can add complexity due to differing requirements or ease of use.

Auto Enrolment

Some firms charge a monthly fee for auto-enrolment updates every three years or the initial registration, while most charge a one-off fee.

Because these are fixed rates and don't happen frequently, we don't have specific KPIs or charge-out rates to share. Two key price points to consider are the **initial registration for auto-enrolment** and the **three-year re-confirmation**.

CIS (Construction Industry Scheme)

Monthly subcontractor submissions are often grouped with the payroll service due to the overlap in PAYE details.

Typical Rates:

- Base rate: £5.00 to £10.00 per subcontractor submission (average: £7.50)

Pricing Factors:

- Average number of subcontractors

Example Formula:

Base Rate x Number of Subcontractors = Monthly Fee

This is very similar to the payroll service so please refer to that example table.

Accounts & Tax Return Services

Accounts and tax return services can vary greatly depending on the type of business, turnover, and complexity of the client's records. We're seeing an increasing trend of firms combining company accounts and corporation tax returns into a single service, as most firms won't perform one without the other. This section covers these combined services as well as other tax-related offerings.

Company Accounts & CT600 (Corporation Tax Return)

A key pricing indicator for this service, which we haven't discussed in depth yet, is **turnaround time**—the ability to charge more to clients who want or need their annual accounts completed quicker than average. For example, a client who requires accounts completed within 4–6 weeks of their year-end could be charged more than a client with a more flexible deadline. Ultimately, you're providing an increased value of service to meet the client's requirements, which justifies a higher fee.

Some firms prefer to charge annually for this service, while others spread the cost monthly throughout the year. More firms are moving towards a monthly model, so that's what we'll focus on here.

Typical Rates:

- Base rate: £20.00 to £500.00 per month, resulting in annual fees of £240.00 to £6,000.00 (Note: Fees vary widely based on turnover, with firms serving clients ranging from nil to £10m annual turnover.)

Pricing Factors:

- Annual Turnover
- Industry Type
- Quality of Records
- Expected Turnaround Time

Example Formula:

Base Rate x Annual Turnover x Industry Type x Quality of Records x Expected Turnaround Time = Monthly Fee

Because there's so many varying factors in this service, I have not provided an example table in this scenario.

Self-Employed Accounts, Partnership Accounts, Charity Accounts

These services can be priced similarly to company accounts, following the same structure of KPIs such as turnover, industry, and quality of records. The monthly base rate typically falls between £40.00 to £500.00, depending on the complexity of the engagement.

SA800 Partnership Tax Returns

Most firms charge a fixed annual amount divided by twelve for partnership tax returns. Some firms, however, incorporate turnover, industry, and turnaround times into their pricing model.

Typical Rates:

- Base rate: £100.00 to £200.00 annually (majority average around £150.00)

Pricing Factors:

- Annual Turnover
- Industry Type
- Quality of Records
- Expected Turnaround Time

Example Formula:

Base Rate x Annual Turnover x Industry Type x Quality of Records x Expected Turnaround Time = Monthly Fee

SA100 Personal Self-Assessment Tax Returns

SA100 Self-Assessments are priced in a variety of ways. Some firms charge a standard fixed fee annually or split over twelve months. Others use a more complex method, charging a starting fee for general information sections and one income type (e.g., employment), with additional fees for extra sections such as dividends, capital gains, or partnerships.

This method ensures more complex returns are charged at a higher rate than simpler ones.

Typical Rates:

- Base rate: £100.00 to £300.00 annually (average total fee: £217.00)

Pricing Factors:

- Number of Returns Required
- Employment
- Self-Employment

- Partnerships
- Dividends
- Pensions
- Foreign Income
- Bank Interest
- Child Benefit
- Other Sections

Example Formula:

Base Rate + Employment + Self-Employment + Partnership + Dividends + Pensions + Foreign Income + Bank Interest + Child Benefit + Other Sections x Number of Returns Required = Annual Fee

The Evolution of Pricing in Our Industry

Pricing within the UK's accounting and bookkeeping sector has undergone a significant transformation over the years. What started as a rigid, hourly-based model has now evolved into a dynamic, client-centred approach that balances efficiency with value. To understand where we are today, it's essential to look back at how pricing practices have developed and what has driven these changes.

The Early Days: Hourly Rates Rule

In the early days of the profession, the pricing model was simple—hourly billing. Accountants and bookkeepers charged clients based on the time spent working on their books. This approach was easy to calculate, transparent in theory, and ensured practitioners were paid for every minute of their efforts.

However, the hourly model had its flaws. Clients often felt disconnected from the true value of the service, focusing solely on the cost rather than the outcomes delivered. Similarly, practitioners found their earning potential capped by the finite number of hours in a day. Over time, it became evident that this model wasn't conducive to fostering strong client relationships or enabling firms to scale sustainably.

The Shift to Fixed Fees

By the late 20th century, firms began to explore fixed-fee pricing. This approach brought predictability for both clients and practitioners. Clients appreciated knowing upfront what they would be charged, while firms could streamline their invoicing and reduce disputes over time sheets. Fixed fees also incentivized efficiency; practitioners who implemented automation or streamlined processes could deliver services faster without compromising profitability.

However, fixed fees were not without their challenges. Many firms struggled to set fees accurately, often underestimating the time and resources required. This sometimes led to resentment, as clients received more value than the fees reflected.

The Advent of Technology: Data-Driven Pricing

The early 2000s marked a turning point with the rise of technology in accounting and bookkeeping. Cloud-based software like Xero, QuickBooks, and Sage revolutionized the way practitioners managed client data. These tools not only streamlined processes but also provided real-time insights into client activity—data that became invaluable for pricing.

Metrics such as transaction volume, payroll size, and the complexity of records could now be used to tailor fees to individual clients. This shift marked the emergence of Key Pricing Indicators (KPIs), allowing firms to align pricing more closely with the workload and value delivered.

The Rise of Value-Based Pricing

In more recent years, the industry has seen a shift towards value-based pricing. This model moves away from charging for time or tasks and instead focuses on the outcomes and benefits clients receive. Whether it's peace of mind, tax savings, or improved cash flow, value-based pricing positions fees as a reflection of the impact practitioners have on their clients' businesses.

Value-based pricing empowers firms to charge for their expertise and the results they deliver, rather than just their effort. It requires a deep understanding of the client's needs and a confident ability to communicate the value being provided.

Modern Challenges and Innovations

Today, pricing in the accounting and bookkeeping industry is more complex—and more exciting—than ever. Firms must navigate an increasingly competitive landscape while adapting to clients' evolving expectations. The shift towards digital tools and automation has introduced efficiency but also heightened pressure to justify fees in a world where basic compliance tasks are increasingly commoditized.

At the same time, advancements in pricing tools, such as Engager.app's pricing calculator, have made it easier for firms to incorporate sophisticated equations and KPIs into their pricing models. Firms can now offer tailored solutions that reflect the unique circumstances of each client, ensuring fairness and profitability.

Lessons from History

The history of pricing in the UK accounting and bookkeeping industry is a testament to the profession's adaptability. From hourly rates to fixed fees, and now to value-based and data-driven models, practitioners have continuously evolved to meet the needs of their clients and the realities of their businesses. The key takeaway? Pricing is not static—it is a dynamic process that requires ongoing reflection, refinement, and responsiveness to change.

As you develop your own pricing strategy, remember the lessons from the past. Embrace innovation, understand the value you provide, and don't be afraid to adapt. The future of pricing in the industry is bright, and with the right approach, you can ensure your firm remains sustainable and profitable for years to come.

Why Pricing is Essential for Firm Sustainability

Setting the right price isn't just about covering your costs or boosting profits; it's about building a sustainable practice that can grow, adapt, and continue to serve your clients effectively.

In many ways, pricing is the bedrock of your firm's long-term stability, ensuring you have the resources to meet evolving client needs, invest in staff and technology, and navigate changes in the market.

Profitability Fuels Growth

Without a solid pricing structure, even the most well-intentioned firm can find itself on shaky ground. Undercharging or failing to adjust fees as your services expand can limit profitability, restricting the resources you need for growth. Profitable pricing allows you to reinvest in the firm—whether that means hiring top talent, investing in essential tools, or improving client offerings. Each of these investments not only strengthens your firm but also enhances the value you deliver to clients, creating a win-win scenario for both parties.

Supports Quality and Consistency

Pricing that accurately reflects the effort involved allows your team to focus on delivering quality rather than cutting corners to save time. When fees are set to support the actual workload and complexity, it ensures that your firm can maintain high standards and deliver consistent results. Over time, clients come to rely on that consistency, trusting that your firm will provide accurate, timely, and proactive service.

Mitigates Client and Service Risk

Low pricing can sometimes attract clients who may undervalue your services or demand more than what they're paying for, creating an imbalance that risks firm resources and staff well-being. By aligning your fees with the true cost and value of your services, you not only attract clients who respect and appreciate your work but also establish boundaries that allow for sustainable client relationships. In the end, clients who understand the value they're receiving are more likely to remain loyal, engaged, and receptive to fee adjustments over time.

Enables Flexibility and Innovation

Sustainable pricing also gives your firm the breathing room to evolve and innovate. Without pressure to chase volume or accept unprofitable engagements, you can prioritize the projects, tools, and processes that improve your efficiency and expand your service offering. This flexibility is essential for staying competitive, especially as the accounting landscape shifts and client needs become more complex. Whether it's implementing new technology, exploring advisory services, or specializing in high-demand niches, a well-priced firm can pivot and respond to new opportunities confidently.

Prepares Your Firm for the Future

Pricing that accounts for inflation, software costs, and changing market demands is a proactive approach to firm management. Regularly reviewing and adjusting your fees not only helps maintain profitability but also keeps your services in line with industry standards. This is crucial for longevity, as it allows you to meet rising costs head-on and ensures you're prepared to sustain your firm through economic fluctuations, regulatory changes, and shifts in client expectations.

In short, pricing isn't just about covering your costs today—it's about ensuring that your firm has the resources, resilience, and readiness to thrive tomorrow. With a sustainable pricing structure, you're creating a foundation that supports growth, quality, client satisfaction, and long-term success.

Software's to Help You Price

As I referred to briefly in the Introduction, there's several software on the market focused on accountants and bookkeepers to help you price more accurately, confidently, and efficiently.

In this chapter we will look software solutions that price and send letters of engagements and proposals and those that can help gather the insights to answer the Key Pricing Indicators questions you set yourself.

I won't be covering every pricing and proposal tool on the market in this chapter, just the main players that we often see recommended by accountants and bookkeepers.

I will try my best to be as neutral as possible in this section and not sway you based on my own opinions of functionality, price, culture, methods used to price etc.

Pricing Software's

First, we will investigate pricing software's these are software's that help you generate a price based on key information, generate a Letter of Engagement and/or proposal document.

Key areas we will consider in this review of software's are:

Pricing model – How you are charged, per user or by the number of clients?

Limit of proposals per month – This is how many clients and prospects you can send proposals and letters of engagement to in a month.

Number of Key pricing Indicators per service – This how many steps and KPIS you can include in a pricing formula for a service.

Support for pricing methods - what pricing methods does the software support? Hourly, monthly, quarterly, annual and tiers.

Supports Catch fees – does the software help you calculate catch up fees? A catch-up fee is when a client joins you part way through their financial year and needs to pay an amount for the fees they would have paid towards their services if they joined you at the start of their financial year.

Engager.app

I know it's the easy one, but let's set the standard, shall we?
Engager provides a free pricing tool and Letter of Engagement
generator free of charge within its Practice Management software.

Pricing Model	By number of clients
Starting Price (Ex VAT)	£9.00
Limit on the number of proposals/LOE's per month	Unlimited
Pricing Calculator Included?	Yes
Number of Key Pricing Indicators per service	Unlimited
Allows Custom Pricing Indicators	Yes
Supports Hourly Rates	Yes
Supports Fixed Monthly Fees?	Yes
Supports Fixed Quarterly Fees?	Yes
Supports Fixed Annual Fees?	Yes
Supports Tier Pricing	No
Supports Catch Up Fees	Yes

Not all Practice Management tools include pricing and letters of
engagement features, and you will need a standalone solution for
your pricing. If for example you use Senta, Karbon, UKU, Xero
Practice Manager or Glide then you will need to consider a
standalone pricing tool.

Bright Manager

Bright Manager is a practice management tool similar to Engager.app, it has a comprehensive set of features to help you run your practice similar to Engager.app.

Pricing Model	By number of users
Starting Price (Ex VAT)	£33.60 Per Month
Limit on the number of proposals/LOE's per month	Unlimited
Pricing Calculator Included?	No
Number of Key Pricing Indicators per service	None
Allows Custom Pricing Indicators	No
Supports Hourly Rates	No
Supports Fixed Monthly Fees?	Yes
Supports Fixed Quarterly Fees?	No
Supports Fixed Annual Fees?	Yes
Supports Tier Pricing	Yes
Supports Catch Up Fees	No

While Bright manager does include Letters of Engagement and the ability to add prices per service it does not provide a calculator so you will need to use this alongside a spreadsheet or another pricing solution to help you calculate the fees to charge.

Bright Propose

Bright propose is Brights standalone pricing solution launched originally as a competitor to GoProposal and Ignition.

Pricing Model	Unlimited Users
Starting Price (Ex VAT)	£50.00 Per Month
Limit on the number of proposals/LOE's per month	5 a month
Pricing Calculator Included?	Yes
Number of Key Pricing Indicators per service	3
Allows Custom Pricing Indicators	No
Supports Hourly Rates	No
Supports Fixed Monthly Fees?	Yes
Supports Fixed Quarterly Fees?	Yes
Supports Fixed Annual Fees?	Yes
Supports Tier Pricing	No
Supports Catch Up Fees	Yes

Another note on the KPI's used in Bright Propose is that you can only use the ones built in by Bright, at the time of publishing this book you cannot add your own Key Pricing Factors.

Go Proposal by Sage

GoProposal and its founder, James Ashford are owed an undeniable debit of gratitude for igniting the rethinking how accountants and bookkeepers price their services.

Until this software became popular charging hourly was the norm and although business coaches were encouraging the industry to modernise it wasn't until GoProposal delivered their tool which made pricing monthly fees quicker and easier that it became more standard to charge monthly fees based on value and transactions etc, not just time in the industry.

Pricing Model	Per User
Starting Price (Ex VAT)	£65.00 Per Month
Limit on the number of proposals/LOE's per month	5 a month
Pricing Calculator Included?	Yes
Number of Key Pricing Indicators per service	5
Allows Custom Pricing Indicators	Yes
Supports Hourly Rates	No
Supports Fixed Monthly Fees?	Yes
Supports Fixed Quarterly Fees?	No
Supports Fixed Annual Fees?	No
Supports Tier Pricing	No
Supports Catch Up Fees	Yes

Ignition

Ignition is a good tool if you want to price using a tier pricing offering such as a bronze, silver and gold type packages where the client chooses one at the time of sign up.

Ignition has a built-in payments solution as well, helping to collect payments for services easily. Ignition is the only solution with this built in while GoProposal integrates with GoCardless and Engager is developing an integration with their latest Partner, Adfin.

For information on Ignition's payment charge rates please refer to their website.

Pricing Model	3 Users, up to 30 Clients
Starting Price (Ex VAT)	£99.00 Per Month
Limit on the number of proposals/LOE's per month	None
Pricing Calculator Included?	No
Number of Key Pricing Indicators per service	None
Allows Custom Pricing Indicators	No
Supports Hourly Rates	No
Supports Fixed Monthly Fees?	Yes
Supports Fixed Quarterly Fees?	Yes
Supports Fixed Annual Fees?	Yes
Supports Tier Pricing	Yes
Supports Catch Up Fees	No

Software's Comparison Table

	Engager	Bright Manager	Bright Propose	GoProposal	Ignition
Pricing Model	By number of clients	By number of users	Unlimited Users	Per User	3 Users, Up to 30 Clients
Starting Price (Ex VAT)	£9.00	£33.60 Per Month	£50.00 Per Month	£65.00 Per Month	£99.00 Per Month
Limit on the number of proposals/LOE's per month	Unlimited	Unlimtied	5 a month	5 a month	None
Pricing Calculator Included?	Yes	No	Yes	Yes	No
Number of Key Pricing Indicators per service	Unlimited	None	3	5	None
Allows Custom Pricing Indicators		No	No	Yes	No
Supports Hourly Rates	Yes	No	Yes	No	No
Supports Fixed Monthly Fees?	Yes	Yes	Yes	Yes	Yes
Supports Fixed Quarterly Fees?	Yes	No	Yes	No	Yes
Supports Fixed Annual Fees?	Yes	Yes	Yes	No	Yes
Supports Tier Pricing	No	Yes	No	No	Yes
Supports Catch Up Fees	Yes	No	Yes	Yes	No

Data Gathering Software's

To be able to price your clients using the methods discussed in this book requires you to have insights to KPIs such as turnover, number of bank transactions, number of purchase invoices etc. Collecting this information and ensuring it's accurate can be time consuming, but the good news is that there are tools available on the market to make collecting this information quickly and accurately easier.

There are two main tools that focus primarily on data analysis which are Xenon and Dext Precision. Both tools link to your Finance Management Solution such as FreeAgent, Quickbooks, Sage and Xero and surfaces the KPI's you want to use for pricing your clients.

Other tools to consider are Syft Analytics which has a module in its reporting tool you can use or Quickbooks which has some insights in its overview tool.

If you want to make pricing more efficient and accurate then tools like the ones above certainly help you achieve that goal.

Common Pricing Pitfalls

Pricing is as much an art as it is a science, and while everyone's approach will differ, there are a few common traps that can catch even the most experienced firms off guard. Knowing these in advance can save you headaches down the line—and keep your pricing where it should be: profitable, practical, and manageable.

Underestimating Workload

It's easy to misjudge the time required for a service, especially when you're eager to win new clients or build strong relationships. But consistently undercharging for the real scope of work can lead to resentment on both sides. If you often find yourself going "above and beyond" without appropriate compensation, it's time to reassess your pricing structure. Remember, it's not about charging the highest fee; it's about ensuring each service brings value to both your firm and your client.

Ignoring Annual Inflation and Cost Increases

Costs rise every year, whether it's wages, software subscriptions, or compliance expenses. If you don't adjust your pricing to keep pace, your margins will erode quietly over time. Consider implementing an annual price review—even a modest increase in line with inflation can help maintain your profitability.

One-Size-Fits-All Pricing

As tempting as it might be to simplify things by applying the same model across all clients, every business has different needs. One size rarely fits all, and clients are often willing to pay more for a tailored approach. Using KPIs like transaction volume or record quality ensures that clients are being charged fairly based on the true cost of serving them.

Over-Reliance on Discounts

Discounts can seem like an easy way to win new business or keep a long-term client happy. But frequent discounts can undermine your credibility and lower the perceived value of your services. If discounts aren't carefully managed, they can put pressure on your margins, making it harder to cover operational costs. Stick to a consistent pricing policy, and let your services speak for themselves.

Neglecting Profitability on "Non-Core" Services

It's easy to focus on getting the pricing right for core services like bookkeeping and payroll, but what about the add-ons? Services such as credit control, VAT submissions, or pension management can be high-value tasks that deserve their own place in your pricing model. Failing to price these adequately can lead to a significant amount of "hidden" work—services you provide but don't necessarily get paid for. Ensure every service you deliver is covered by an appropriate fee so that nothing slips through the cracks.

Overlooking the Client's Perspective

Your pricing model is more than just numbers on a page—it's a reflection of your firm's professionalism and confidence. If clients understand the logic behind your fees, they're more likely to see the value and less likely to question it. Take the time to explain how KPIs, quality of records, and frequency impact the fee. Clear, upfront communication can prevent pricing disputes and help clients feel they're getting true value from your service.

Industry-Specific Pricing Challenges

Pricing in the accounting and bookkeeping field is rarely one-size-fits-all, and this is even more evident when you're working with clients across a variety of industries. Each industry brings unique challenges, regulations, and complexities that can impact pricing structures, and the time invested. Understanding these nuances and building them into your pricing strategy can set you apart and ensure you're charging in line with the effort required. Here are some key industry-specific challenges to consider:

Regulation-Heavy Industries

Example Industries: Financial services, healthcare, construction Pricing Challenge: Clients in regulation-heavy sectors typically demand more compliance work, regular checks, and reporting to meet legal standards. This requires additional time, specialized knowledge, and sometimes external audits—all of which increase the workload and risk level.

Pricing Insight: Consider building a "compliance factor" into your base rate or charging a separate fee for tasks linked to regulatory requirements. For example, you might increase fees for industries where you'll need to invest more time in compliance reporting or specialized training.

Seasonal Businesses

Example Industries: Hospitality, retail, agriculture

Pricing Challenge: These businesses see fluctuations in their bookkeeping needs depending on the season. Retailers may need more attention during holiday seasons, while agriculture businesses experience a similar surge during harvest periods. This creates uneven workloads and can strain resources during peak times.

Pricing Insight: Implement a seasonal pricing model or retainers that allow for high-activity periods. Alternatively, consider a "surge fee" for the months where service requirements spike. Transparent communication around these fluctuations and how they impact fees can also improve client understanding.

High-Volume Transaction Clients

Example Industries: E-commerce, manufacturing, logistics

Pricing Challenge: In high-transaction environments, volume is king. These clients often deal with many invoices, transactions, and inventory adjustments that demand time and attention. Automated tools can ease some of the burden, but high-volume clients still require a solid structure to accommodate the workload.

Pricing Insight: Use transaction-based pricing to scale fees alongside volume, and consider an additional "efficiency factor" that rewards clients who maintain clean, well-organized records. For these clients, more frequent service reviews and workload-based fees can be beneficial to ensure fair compensation.

Clients with Extensive Payroll Needs

Example Industries: Retail, food service, manufacturing

Pricing Challenge: Companies with a high number of employees, variable hours, and multiple pay types require extensive payroll support. Processing payroll for these clients can be time-intensive, particularly for industries with seasonal staff turnover or extensive benefits administration.

Pricing Insight: Create a payroll pricing tier that adjusts based on the number of employees and complexity of payroll (such as salaried versus hourly and benefits administration). Engager's pricing tools can help manage variable payroll pricing by incorporating custom equations, ensuring that each service is billed accurately and fairly.

High-Touch Service Industries

Example Industries: Legal, consulting, professional services

Pricing Challenge: Clients in professional services typically expect high-touch, advisory-focused support rather than simple transactional work. These clients often value the insights provided by their accountant or bookkeeper and may rely on you for ongoing financial guidance and strategic input.

Pricing Insight: Emphasize the advisory aspect in your pricing by incorporating "value-added" pricing elements. This may mean establishing advisory fees or premium pricing structures for clients who benefit most from strategy sessions, tax planning, or regular financial health check-ins. Being upfront about these added services and their fees can help set clear expectations.

By proactively addressing these industry-specific challenges, you can tailor your pricing to reflect the true value and effort of your services, while also ensuring fair and sustainable rates. Ultimately, factoring in industry dynamics helps not only your bottom line but also reinforces your role as a strategic partner who understands the nuances of your clients' businesses.

Value-Added Pricing: Focusing on Impact

Value-based pricing might seem like just another industry buzzword, but it's one of the most transformative strategies in your pricing toolkit. Unlike traditional models that rely on hours worked or tasks completed, value-based pricing places emphasis on the unique benefits you deliver to your clients' businesses. It's about recognizing the impact of your expertise and confidently assigning a fee that reflects that value.

Moving from Cost to Value

Traditional pricing models, like hourly or daily rates, focus on the cost of delivering a service—how much time it takes or how much effort is involved. Value-based pricing flips this approach on its head, concentrating instead on the results your services achieve for your clients.

For example, while preparing a set of accounts may only take a few hours, the true value lies in what those accounts provide: actionable insights, peace of mind, and compliance with HMRC requirements. Similarly, automating a client's payroll system isn't just about saving you time—it's about giving your client a streamlined process that ensures accuracy and employee satisfaction. When you frame your fees around these outcomes, you create a direct link between your service and the client's success.

Discovering the Unique Value in Your Services

Every service you provide has "value drivers"—specific outcomes or advantages that your clients benefit from. These might include saving time, reducing risks, increasing profitability, or delivering strategic insights. By identifying these drivers, you can justify fees that reflect the real benefits your services bring.

Let's use bookkeeping as an example. While the task itself may involve processing transactions and reconciling accounts, the true value lies in the bigger picture: enabling better cash flow management, supporting timely decision-making, and fostering compliance. When you highlight these elements during pricing discussions, your clients will start to see your role as essential to their business success—not just a cost on their profit and loss statement.

Shaping the Conversation Around Results

Value-based pricing isn't just about what you charge—it's about how you communicate it. Shifting the conversation away from tasks and towards results is key. Instead of telling a client, "I'll manage your bookkeeping for £X per month," say, "With my bookkeeping service, you'll have real-time financial data at your fingertips, empowering you to make confident decisions and achieve your goals."

This change in language reinforces the idea that your services are an investment, not an expense. When clients understand the tangible and intangible benefits they'll receive, objections to pricing become less about cost and more about value.

Backing Up Value with Data

Clients appreciate transparency, and being able to quantify your value with metrics is an excellent way to build trust. Tools like Engager.app allow you to track service performance and gather data that demonstrates your impact. For instance, if your process reduces a client's manual workload by 10 hours a week, calculate the equivalent monetary value of that time. If your tax planning saves them thousands annually, make sure they know it. These figures don't just justify your pricing—they elevate your role from service provider to indispensable partner.

Start Small, Scale Gradually

Transitioning to value-based pricing doesn't have to happen all at once. Start with a single service or client segment. Use this as an opportunity to test your pricing structure and refine how you communicate value. Gather feedback and assess how well your clients understand the link between your service and their success. Over time, you'll find yourself building a pricing model that's both profitable and aligned with the needs of your firm and your clients.

A Long-Term Strategy for Growth

Value-based pricing isn't a one-off exercise. As your firm evolves and your expertise deepens, your pricing should reflect the growing impact of your services. Regularly revisit your Key Pricing Indicators (KPIs) and update your pricing model to stay aligned with client needs and industry trends. Think of value-based pricing as a partnership—it grows with your business and strengthens your client relationships.

By committing to value-based pricing, you're not just charging for the work you do; you're highlighting the difference you make. In the end, that's what sets sustainable, client-focused firms apart from the rest.

Advanced Pricing Insights

Once you've mastered the fundamentals, there's always room to take pricing strategies further—especially as your firm grows and you refine your approach. Advanced pricing is about moving beyond traditional models, looking deeper into client value, and embracing the latest tech tools to help set and adjust fees with precision. Here are a few insights that can help you elevate your pricing game.

Segmenting Your Client Base

Not all clients are the same, so why should they be priced the same? Client segmentation allows you to categorise clients based on factors like industry, business size, or complexity of services needed. By creating categories, you can offer tailored pricing that better reflects the workload and value for each group. For instance, you may develop a pricing range for small start-ups versus established companies with higher compliance needs. Segmenting allows you to set price points that align with the unique needs and profitability of each group, ensuring every client feels they're paying the right price for the right service.

Action Steps:

Step 1: Identify key client characteristics that impact pricing (e.g., industry, size, compliance needs).

Step 2: Create client segments based on these characteristics and outline typical services or workload for each.

Step 3: Set tiered pricing ranges for each segment, tailored to reflect workload, risk, or complexity.

Utilising Data for Pricing Decisions

Data is becoming one of the most valuable assets for firms fine-tuning their pricing. Advanced tools and software (like Engager's pricing calculator) allow you to gather and analyse data on how long services take, which types of tasks are most time-intensive, and even which clients contribute most to your bottom line. By tracking time, service frequency, and workload through data, you can identify where current pricing may be leaving money on the table—and adjust accordingly.

Action Steps:

Step 1: Identify the key data points to track (e.g., hours per service, service frequency, client profitability).

Step 2: Set up a basic tracking system, whether in Engager, Excel, or another tool.

Step 3: Regularly review the data (monthly, quarterly) to spot where pricing may need adjustment due to higher workloads or increased time investment.

Considering Value-Based Add-Ons

For clients seeking a bit more from your services, value-based add-ons can be a great way to offer additional services at an appropriate price. Think beyond standard packages and consider what additional support could benefit clients, such as monthly financial coaching, cash flow forecasting, or advisory sessions. These add-ons allow you to increase revenue while delivering tailored services that clients find genuinely helpful. Each additional service should come with its own pricing equation, built to reflect the specific work and client benefits involved.

Action Steps:

Step 1: List the common challenges clients face that your firm can solve with additional support (e.g., monthly cash flow reviews, tax planning).

Step 2: Design "add-on packages" around these solutions with clear pricing and benefits.

Step 3: Communicate the add-ons during initial client discussions, showing how these extras add value.

Dynamic Pricing with BODMAS and Custom Equations

Advanced pricing tools, like Engager's calculator, make it possible to go beyond basic calculations by enabling dynamic pricing. With BODMAS-based equations, you can combine multiple KPIs into a more complex formula that adjusts prices based on multiple factors simultaneously. For instance, instead of a flat monthly rate for payroll, you can incorporate variables like the number of employees, pay frequency, and complexity of tasks to calculate a rate that automatically reflects the true workload.

Action Steps:

Step 1: Choose a few complex services (e.g., payroll or VAT returns) where factors like transaction volume, client size, and frequency significantly impact workload.

Step 2: Break down the equation for each service using BODMAS, and test it in a tool like Engager's advanced pricing mode.

Step 3: Use Engager to automate these calculations so they can be applied consistently across clients.

Embracing Automation and Efficiency to Increase Margins

Finally, consider using automation to keep your processes lean and your margins high. Automation tools—whether for transaction categorization, document management, or payroll processing—can save considerable time, allowing you to take on more clients without increasing your workload. By building automation into your workflows, you'll be able to increase the value you deliver while keeping costs down, giving you more flexibility to price competitively or increase profit margins. And as your efficiency increases, you may even consider passing some of those savings back to clients as loyalty rewards, building trust and long-term relationships.

Action Steps:
Step 1: Identify repetitive tasks where automation tools (like bank reconciliation software or invoicing) could replace manual work.
Step 2: Select a tool that integrates well with your practice and consider its cost relative to time savings.
Step 3: Implement automation gradually, starting with one task at a time, to ensure smooth adoption.

Positioning Your Fees in the Initial Engagement

Introducing fees to a potential client is about more than just naming a price; it's an opportunity to demonstrate the value and expertise your firm brings. When done right, the fee discussion becomes a natural part of your initial engagement process—one that feels less like "selling" and more like setting the foundation for a successful partnership. Here's how to position your fees with confidence and clarity from the start:

Set Expectations Early

Don't let fees be the elephant in the room. By discussing fees early in the engagement, you're setting the tone for a transparent and professional relationship. Rather than waiting until the end of the proposal or onboarding process, mention early on that you take a tailored, client-centric approach to pricing. For example, you could say, "We'll work together to ensure our services and fees are the right fit for your needs." This positions your fees as part of a customised solution rather than a one-size-fits-all cost.

Focus on the Benefits, Not Just the Numbers

Before diving into the details of fees, emphasise what clients will gain by working with you. Your expertise, proactive support, and dedication to understanding their business goals are all benefits worth mentioning. For instance, instead of saying, "Our bookkeeping fee is £X per month," try, "With our bookkeeping services, you'll have up-to-date financials, streamlined reporting, and a clear picture of your cash flow—ready whenever you need it to make informed decisions." When clients see the benefits first, the fee naturally becomes a reflection of the value they're receiving.

Be Transparent and Straightforward

When it comes time to discuss fees, avoid jargon and be as clear as possible. Describe what's included in each service and outline any key pricing indicators that influence the rate, such as transaction volume or record quality. Transparency reduces ambiguity and helps clients understand exactly what they're paying for. Remember, the goal is for clients to feel assured that they're getting value for their investment—so be open about the reasons behind your fees.

Offer Context with Examples

Sometimes, clients need a bit of context to fully appreciate your fees. Sharing examples of typical pricing for similar clients can help put your fees into perspective. For instance, you could say, "For clients of your size, our bookkeeping fees typically range between £X and £Y, depending on the complexity of the records." This approach normalises the fee and lets clients know they're not the only ones investing at that level.

Reinforce Value with Flexibility

While it's important to stand by your fees, some clients may still need reassurance. Offer flexibility by explaining how your services and fees can adapt over time to match their changing needs. For example, "As your business grows, we'll adjust our support to ensure you're getting the right level of service without overpaying for unnecessary tasks." This positions you as a partner who's committed to delivering ongoing value, rather than just a service provider with a fixed price tag.

Close with Confidence

Lastly, confidence is key. If you believe in the value you bring, clients are far more likely to see it too. Closing the fee conversation with assurance, such as "We're excited to bring this level of expertise and support to your business," reinforces your worth. It's not about apologising for the price; it's about making it clear that the fee reflects the quality, dedication, and value they can expect from your firm.

Adapting Your Pricing Over Time

In the world of accounting and bookkeeping, flexibility and adaptability in pricing aren't just nice-to-haves; they're essential for long-term success. Market dynamics shift, client needs evolve, and the value of your expertise deepens as your firm grows.

Adapting your pricing over time not only helps you stay aligned with industry standards but ensures your fees reflect the real value you deliver to clients.

Annual Review of Base Rates

Just as you'd recommend clients review their finances regularly, it's crucial to reassess your base rates annually. Inflation, rising software costs, and changes in compliance requirements all impact your operating costs. An annual review ensures that your rates stay in line with these factors, protecting your firm's profitability.

Tip: Build this review into your pricing model from the outset. Communicate to clients that a yearly adjustment is part of your commitment to delivering reliable, high-quality service, reflecting the true costs of doing business.

Evolve with Industry Changes

Tax legislation, software updates, and the growth of digital accounting all impact the work required for specific services. These industry shifts often bring opportunities for added efficiencies—but they can also create additional complexities. Adapting your pricing to reflect these shifts is essential to stay competitive and relevant.

Tip: Regularly review any new regulatory requirements or software innovations that affect your services. As they add value or complexity to your offerings, adjust your rates to keep fees fair, while also accurately reflecting your expertise.

Stay Flexible and Open to Feedback

Finally, a sustainable pricing strategy isn't static—it's responsive. Remain open to client feedback and be prepared to review your approach if it's no longer supporting the needs of your firm or clients. Pricing should ultimately work as a tool that supports your firm's goals and reflects the value you bring.

Tip: Consider running a yearly client feedback survey, focusing on service quality and perceived value. It can be a powerful way to ensure that your pricing continues to be fair, competitive, and reflective of your firm's strengths.

In the end, adapting your pricing over time is about ensuring your firm remains profitable, relevant, and highly valued. By staying proactive and responsive, your pricing can keep pace with your firm's growth and continue to reflect the ever-expanding value you offer to clients.

Communicating Price Increases

As your firm grows and the cost of doing business evolves, adjusting your prices is part of keeping your services profitable and sustainable. But communicating these increases to clients can feel daunting, even if you know they're necessary. The key is to handle it with transparency, confidence, and a focus on the value you're bringing to the client. After all, a well-informed client is far more likely to appreciate why an increase is happening and see it as a reflection of your commitment to their business.

Set Expectations from the Start

When engaging a new client, be upfront about your approach to price reviews. Let them know that you periodically review your fees to account for inflation, software cost increases, and the evolving complexity of work. This should also be documented in your terms of business, which the client agrees to when signing the initial Letter of Engagement. Setting this expectation early helps reduce resistance when it's time for a fee review.

Timing is Everything

The timing of a price increase can make all the difference. Avoid surprising clients with an unexpected increase in the middle of their busiest season or at tax deadlines. Instead, aim to give a reasonable lead time—ideally three months—so they can adjust their budgets and prepare for the new rate. Annual reviews are an ideal time for price adjustments, as they feel like a natural part of the ongoing client relationship.

Be Transparent and Clear

When communicating an increase, avoid vague explanations. Be upfront about the reasons behind the adjustment. It could be a response to rising operational costs, industry changes, or even additional value you're delivering. For example, "With inflation affecting the costs of software, compliance, and other resources we use to support your business, we're adjusting our fees to continue delivering a high standard of service."

Emphasise the Value

Clients need to understand that a price increase isn't just about covering costs; it's about continuing to enhance the value they get from your services. Rather than focusing on the fee itself, draw attention to the outcomes they experience because of your work. For instance, highlight your proactive support in keeping their finances in order, handling compliance seamlessly, or providing insights that help them make informed business decisions.

Personalise When Possible

If possible, take the time to personalise your communication for long-standing clients. A quick email or phone call explaining the new rate and reiterating your commitment to their success can go a long way. Make it clear that their business matters to you, and that the increase reflects your dedication to continuing to support them at the highest level.

Reassure with Options

Reassurance can go a long way when introducing changes. Consider including options, such as a phased approach to the new rate or a breakdown of services. This doesn't mean offering discounts but rather giving clients the chance to understand what's involved in the service and how they can maximise value. For example, "If you'd like to review your current package or look at options, we're here to help ensure you're getting the most from our services."

Finish on a Positive Note

Always end with a positive, forward-looking message. Remind clients of your commitment to their growth and success and reassure them that your focus is on delivering ongoing value.

Closing with confidence and positivity can reinforce your position as a valuable partner to their business.

Below is an example email/letter template you could send to your client after the meeting/call about the fee review with the new fee details

Subject: Service Fee Update for [Year]

Dear [first name],

As part of our commitment to providing the highest standard of service, we periodically review our pricing structure. Due to [reasons for increase, e.g., inflation, software costs], we are implementing a fee adjustment.

Effective [date], your new fee for [service] will be [new fee]. This adjustment reflects our ongoing dedication to delivering excellent results and support for your business.

We appreciate your understanding and look forward to continuing our partnership. Should you have any questions, please feel free to reach out.

Best regards,

[User]

[Firm]

Dealing with Pricing Objections

When it comes to pricing, objections are a natural part of the process. Whether it's a potential client questioning your initial proposal or an existing client responding to a price adjustment, objections aren't a sign of failure—they're an opportunity to demonstrate the value of your services and strengthen your client relationships. In this chapter, we'll explore how to navigate pricing objections with confidence and professionalism.

Understanding the Root of Objections

Before you can address a pricing objection, it's essential to understand what's driving it. Objections typically fall into one of the following categories:

Perceived Lack of Value: Clients may not fully understand the scope of your services or the benefits they'll gain. This is often a sign that the value hasn't been clearly communicated.

Budget Constraints: Particularly common for small businesses, budget concerns can lead to pushback on fees, regardless of the value you offer.

Comparisons to Competitors: Clients may reference lower-priced quotes from other firms, assuming all services are equal.

Fear of Change: When repricing existing clients, the objection often stems from discomfort with change or a perceived loss of the status quo.

By understanding these root causes, you can tailor your response to address the specific concern and build trust.

Strategies for Addressing Pricing Objections

Lead with Empathy: Start by listening to the client's concerns without interruption. Acknowledge their perspective with statements like, "I understand why this might seem like a big change," or, "Budget constraints can be challenging, especially for businesses looking to grow."

Empathy shows you're not dismissive of their concerns, setting a collaborative tone for the conversation.

Reaffirm the Value: Many objections arise from a lack of clarity about the value your services provide. Reiterate how your work helps their business, emphasizing outcomes rather than tasks. For example:

Instead of saying, "We reconcile your bank accounts," frame it as, "Our bank reconciliation ensures you always have an accurate financial picture, empowering you to make confident decisions." Use real examples or metrics where possible: "Clients in your industry who use our VAT services typically save 10-15 hours per month in compliance time."

Break Down the Costs: Help clients see what they're paying for by breaking down your fees. Show them how your pricing aligns with the scope of work and outcomes. For example:
"The monthly fee of £300 covers all payroll processing for your 10 employees, including compliance checks, payslips, and pension submissions."
A detailed breakdown can often demystify your fees and reduce sticker shock.

Address Comparisons Head-On: If a client references a competitor's lower pricing, avoid disparaging the competitor. Instead, focus on highlighting what sets you apart. For example:
"While other firms may offer lower rates, we include features like real-time reporting and dedicated support, ensuring you're never left in the dark when you need help."
Transparency about the difference in services helps clients see why you're worth the investment.

Offer Options Without Undermining Your Value: For clients with genuine budget concerns, consider offering tiered options that reduce scope without reducing your rate. For example:

"If monthly VAT support feels like too much right now, we could explore quarterly submissions to align with your budget."

This keeps the door open for future growth while maintaining the integrity of your pricing.

Reframe Price Increases as Opportunities: When repricing existing clients, position the increase as part of your commitment to delivering top-tier services. For example:

"Over the past year, we've introduced new tools that streamline your payroll process and reduce errors. To continue providing this level of service, we've adjusted our pricing."

By focusing on improvements and benefits, clients are less likely to feel penalized by the change.

Handling Persistent Objections

Despite your best efforts, some objections may persist. When this happens, it's essential to maintain your professionalism and boundaries:

Know When to Walk Away: Not every client is the right fit for your firm. If a potential client is fixated on price without recognizing value, they may not be the ideal partner for your services. Politely decline with confidence:

"It seems like we may not be the best fit for your needs, but I'd be happy to recommend a colleague who might align better with your budget."

Stand Firm on Value for Existing Clients: Long-term clients may resist price increases out of habit, but undervaluing your work can hurt your business. Stand firm while showing flexibility in other areas:

"I understand the adjustment may feel significant, but it reflects the time and expertise we dedicate to ensuring your accounts are handled with precision. Let's review the scope to make sure it aligns with your goals."

Keep the Door Open: If a potential client declines your services due to price, leave the relationship on good terms. Often, businesses realize the value of quality support after encountering challenges elsewhere. Follow up periodically to check in.

Turning Objections into Relationships

Handled well, pricing objections can become opportunities to build trust and deepen relationships. By listening, educating, and standing confidently behind your pricing, you demonstrate your commitment to delivering value—not just in financial terms but in the trust, expertise, and partnership you bring to the table.

Every objection is a chance to refine your approach and strengthen your firm's reputation as a provider of essential, impactful services. When you approach these conversations with clarity, empathy, and professionalism, you'll find that many objections dissolve into appreciation for the value you deliver.

Conclusion

In summary, pricing is a journey, not a fixed formula.

While this book provides insights, examples, and foundational principles, the most successful pricing strategy is one that aligns with the unique dynamics of your firm and clients. Use this as a framework to guide your own approach, adapting as your experience and client base evolve.

With Engager's tools and community support, you're well-equipped to approach pricing with confidence, clarity, and the assurance that you're building a sustainable and profitable practice. Embrace it, refine it, and most importantly, make it work for you.

To see how you can use these methods in practice within Engager.app I would suggest visiting the Engager Help Guide https://help.engager.app and have a look at our guides and videos there including the video entitled "pricing deep dive" where I show you how to build the pricing and key pricing indicators.

Further support in implementing your own pricing methods can be found on our weekly live sessions which we run at 7.30pm every Wednesday on zoom, these can be signed up to from our help centre.

Remember, pricing should be flexible, adapting to industry changes, inflation, and the unique value you bring to clients. With Engager.app's tools and community support, you're well-equipped to approach pricing with confidence, clarity, and the assurance that you're building a sustainable and profitable practice. Embrace it, refine it, and most importantly, make it work for you.

One Final Piece of Advice

Your first attempt at pricing—or in fact, your first attempt at anything in business—is going to be better than no attempt at all. Waiting until your pricing is "perfect" will lead to never launching because it will never feel perfect. Engager knows even the most well-structured pricing process won't fit every scenario, which is why the pricing tool generates a "suggested fee" that you can adjust before finalising your Letter of Engagement.

Don't be afraid to start, experiment, and iterate. Pricing is a journey, and each step will bring you closer to a model that works best for your firm and clients.

Glossary of Terms

Annual Turnover: The total income generated by a business over a year before any deductions. In pricing, turnover can be a Key Pricing Indicator (KPI) to help set fees based on the client's business scale.

Base Rate (BR): The starting fee for a service, charged per unit (e.g., per document, per month, or per transaction). The base rate is adjusted using various KPIs to determine the final fee.

BODMAS: A mathematical principle used to organize calculations: Brackets, Orders (powers and roots), Division and Multiplication, Addition and Subtraction. Engager.app advanced pricing mode supports BODMAS to help create complex pricing formulas.

Client Segmentation: The practice of categorizing clients based on characteristics like business size, industry, or service complexity. Segmenting clients helps create tailored pricing that reflects the workload and value for each group.

Dynamic Pricing: A flexible pricing model where fees adjust according to real-time variables, such as workload changes or client needs. Dynamic pricing often uses KPIs and BODMAS calculations to create more precise fees.

Engagement: The formal agreement between a firm and a client to provide specific services. This includes setting fees, expectations, and scope of work.

Key Pricing Indicator (KPI): A piece of information or metric that influences the price of a service, such as the number of transactions, frequency of service, quality of records, or annual turnover. KPIs help tailor pricing based on the unique requirements of each client.

Letter of Engagement (LOE): A document that outlines the services, terms, and pricing agreed upon between the firm and client. The LOE sets expectations and serves as a formal contract.

Pricing Calculator: A tool within Engager.app that helps users set fees by calculating base rates and KPIs. The calculator includes a simple pricing wizard for basic pricing and an advanced mode for complex formulas.

Pricing Equation: The formula used to calculate the final fee for a service. A typical pricing equation includes the base rate multiplied by relevant KPIs (e.g., Base Rate x Transaction Volume x Quality of Records = Final Fee).

Profitability: A measure of how much profit a service or client generates for the firm. Regularly reviewing profitability ensures that pricing remains sustainable and fair.

Value-Based Pricing: A pricing model that focuses on the value a service provides to the client, rather than just the time or effort required. Value-based pricing allows firms to charge fees that reflect the outcomes clients experience.

Value Driver: An element of a service that provides unique value to a client, such as time savings, compliance support, or financial insights. Value drivers justify higher fees by emphasizing the specific benefits clients gain.

Printed in Great Britain
by Amazon

52348387R00059